A Guide for Using

I Heard the Owl Call My Name

in the Classroom

Based on the novel written by Margaret Craven

This guide written by Mari Lu Robbins

Teacher Created Materials, Inc.
6421 Industry Way
Westminster, CA 92683
www.teachercreated.com
©1994 Teacher Created Materials, Inc.
Reprinted, 1999
Made in U.S.A.
ISBN 1-55734-520-1

Edited by
Janet Cain

Illustrated by
Kris Sexton

Cover Art by
Theresa Wright

Table of Contents

Introduction

Good books are wonderful! They stimulate our imagination, inform our minds, inspire our higher selves, and fill our time with magic! With good books, we are never lonely or bored. And a good book only gets better with time, because each reading brings us new meaning. Each new story is a treasure to cherish forever.

In *Literature Units*, we take great care to select books that will become treasured friends for life.

Teachers using this unit will find the following features to supplement their own valuable ideas.

- Sample Lesson Plans

- Pre-reading Activities

- A Biographical Sketch of the Author

- A Book Summary

- Vocabulary Lists and Suggested Vocabulary Activities

- Chapters grouped for study, with each section including:
  - *quizzes*
  - *hands-on projects*
  - *cooperative learning activities*
  - *cross-curricular connections*
  - *extensions into the reader's own life*

- Post-reading Activities

- Book Report Ideas

- Research Ideas

- A Culminating Activity

- Three Different Options for Unit Tests

- Bibliography

- Answer Key

We are confident that this unit will be a valuable addition to your literature planning, and that as you use our ideas, your students will learn to treasure the stories to which you introduce them.

Sample Lesson Plan

Each of the lessons suggested below can take from one to several days to complete.

LESSON 1
- Introduce and complete some or all of the pre-reading ideas found on page 5.
- Read "About the Author" with your students. (page 6)
- Read the book summary with your students. (page 7)
- Read and discuss the North American Indian myths with your students. (pages 13-15)
- Introduce the vocabulary list for Section 1. (page 8)

LESSON 2
- Read Chapters 1 and 2. As you read, place the vocabulary words in the context of the story and discuss their meanings.
- Choose a vocabulary activity. (page 9)
- Design a totem pole. (page 11)
- Complete an anticipation guide. (page 12)
- Identify the lessons taught in the three myths. (pages 13-15)
- Begin "Reading Response Journals." (page 16)
- Administer Section 1 quiz. (page 10)
- Introduce the vocabulary list for Section 2. (page 8)

LESSON 3
- Read Chapters 3-7. Place the vocabulary words in context and discuss their meanings.
- Choose a vocabulary activity. (page 9)
- Learn to bake bread. (page 18)
- Portray a character from the book. (page 19)
- Learn how a fable told within the story is used to teach a lesson. (page 20)
- Write a diamond poem. (page 21)
- Administer Section 2 quiz. (page 17)
- Introduce the vocabulary list for Section 3. (page 8)

LESSON 4
- Read chapters 8-11. Place the vocabulary words in context and discuss their meanings.
- Choose a vocabulary activity. (page 9)
- Make papier-mâché masks. (page 23)
- Develop the ability to tell a story. (page 24)
- Learn about the geography of Kingcome and its surroundings. (page 25)
- Compare characters feelings. (page 26)
- Administer Section 3 quiz. (page 22)
- Introduce the vocabulary words for Section 4. (page 8)

LESSON 5
- Read chapters 12-17. Place the vocabulary words in context and discuss their meanings.
- Choose a vocabulary activity. (page 9)
- Design a canoe. (page 28)
- Supply the clues to a crossword puzzle. (page 29)
- Learn how to use more precise words when writing. (page 30)
- Identify the qualities you think help a person earn respect. (page 31)
- Administer Section 4 quiz. (page 27)
- Introduce the vocabulary list for Section 5. (page 8)

LESSON 6
- Read chapters 18-23. Place the vocabulary words in context and discuss their meanings.
- Choose a vocabulary activity. (page 9)
- Bake a volcano. (page 33)
- Build a model of a mountain. (page 34)
- Conduct a survey to identify people's beliefs about numbers. (page 35)
- Write an obituary or a eulogy. (page 36)
- Administer the Section 5 quiz. (page 32)

LESSON 7
- Discuss any question your students might have about the story. (page 37)
- Assign book reports and research projects. (pages 38 and 39)
- Begin work on culminating activity. (pages 40 and 41)

LESSON 8
- Administer unit tests 1,2, and/or 3. (pages 42, 43 and 44)
- Discuss the test answers and possibilities.
- Discuss the students' enjoyment of the book.
- Redistribute the anticipation guide, and ask students if they have changed any of their opinions. (page 12)
- Provide a list of related reading for your students. (page 46)

LESSON 9
- Complete the culminating activity by celebrating the storytelling potlatch. (pages 40 and 41)

Before the Book

Your students will improve their comprehension and enhance their enjoyment of *I Heard the Owl Call My Name* if they have some prior knowledge about the culture described in the book. By using some general pre-reading strategies students can better understand the concepts presented in the literature. Here are some ideas that may work well with your class.

1.   Have students predict what the story might be about by hearing the title.

2.   Ask students to predict what the story might be about by looking at the cover illustration.

3.   Have students complete the anticipation guide on page 12, and discuss the answers. Save the guide so students can refer to it after completing the book.

4.   Discuss various cultures students have encountered in stories they have read or heard.

5.   Discuss how stories and group histories once had to be passed down by word of mouth in what we call the "oral tradition." Ask students if they think people used to know more about their family history than they do today.

6.   Define mythology and folklore. Ask students if they know any North American Indian myths or legends, or Greek or Roman myths. Ask what part these stories played in the lives of the people who told them.

7.   Read the myths which came from the Indians of the Northwest on pages 13-15. Discuss these stories and what they may have meant to the people who believed them. Ask students: What kind of relationship did these people have with nature, and how does it differ from your own? What kinds of gods did the Indians seem to have? Why were the Indians' gods an important part of their lives? What did the people believe would happen if they behaved in a way that displeased the gods?

8.   Have students answer these questions.

     What would it be like if you:

     — learned you had only three years left to live?

     — moved to a part of the world which was totally different than anything you've ever known?

     — found yourself living with people who have a primitive lifestyle?

     — decided to devote your life to helping others?

About the Author

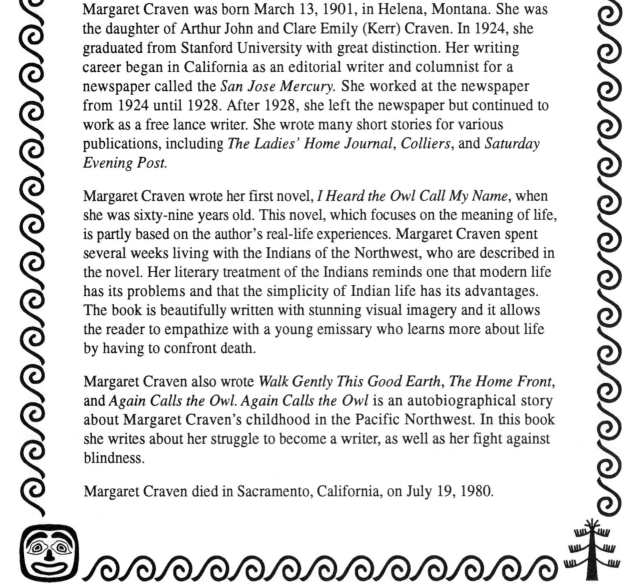

Margaret Craven was born March 13, 1901, in Helena, Montana. She was the daughter of Arthur John and Clare Emily (Kerr) Craven. In 1924, she graduated from Stanford University with great distinction. Her writing career began in California as an editorial writer and columnist for a newspaper called the *San Jose Mercury*. She worked at the newspaper from 1924 until 1928. After 1928, she left the newspaper but continued to work as a free lance writer. She wrote many short stories for various publications, including *The Ladies' Home Journal*, *Colliers*, and *Saturday Evening Post*.

Margaret Craven wrote her first novel, *I Heard the Owl Call My Name*, when she was sixty-nine years old. This novel, which focuses on the meaning of life, is partly based on the author's real-life experiences. Margaret Craven spent several weeks living with the Indians of the Northwest, who are described in the novel. Her literary treatment of the Indians reminds one that modern life has its problems and that the simplicity of Indian life has its advantages. The book is beautifully written with stunning visual imagery and it allows the reader to empathize with a young emissary who learns more about life by having to confront death.

Margaret Craven also wrote *Walk Gently This Good Earth*, *The Home Front*, and *Again Calls the Owl*. *Again Calls the Owl* is an autobiographical story about Margaret Craven's childhood in the Pacific Northwest. In this book she writes about her struggle to become a writer, as well as her fight against blindness.

Margaret Craven died in Sacramento, California, on July 19, 1980.

I Heard the Owl Call My Name

by Margaret Craven

(Dell, 1973, 1980);
(Available in Canada from Doubleday Dell Seal;
in UK from Pan Books; and in AUS from Transworld Pub.)

Mark Brian does not know when he takes his first assignment as a vicar that it will be his last. Being only twenty-seven years old, he never stops to consider his own mortality. He plans for the future, yet he has only two years to live. He has so much to learn about life and so little time in which to learn it.

Mark is sent to be a vicar at an Indian village in a remote area of the Pacific Northwest. It seems to be a land without time, where life and death walk hand-in-hand. When Mark arrives, he thinks the villagers, who are his congregation, all look alike. He believes they lead a simple life and are generally ignorant about the ways of the world.

As time passes, the reader comes to know the village as Mark Brian does. Mark learns what the bishop means when he says that *'The Indian knows his village and feels for his village as no white man for his country, his town, or even for his own bit of land. His village is not the strip of land.... The myths are the village and the winds and the rains. The river is the village, and the black and white killer whales....The village is the salmon who comes up the river to spawn, the seal who follows the salmon..., the bluejay.... The village is the talking bird, the owl, who calls the name of the man who is going to die, and the silver-tipped grizzly who ambles into the village....The fifty-foot totem by the church is the village, and the Cedar-man who stands at the bottom holding up the eagle, the wolf and the raven!'*

Mark grows to love the people, and they grow to love him. He sees that the Indians are not at all the same, that each is unique. He realizes that the Indians' lifestyles, which he thought were so simplistic, are really very complex. Mark does everything he can to help and comfort the people. They, in turn, teach him the meaning of life.

Vocabulary Lists

SECTION 1
(Chapters 1-2)

literally	parish	lectern
selvage	stowed	gesture
bilge	toque	canon
vicar	cassock	aft
dorsal	barnacle	discern
potlatch	jaunty	trestle
vicarage	muskeg	disperse
tremulous	inanimate	reminiscence
garrulous		

SECTION 2
(Chapters 3-7)

confabulation	orator	dank
gentility	matriarch	sundry
tarpaulin	descended	surplice
moor	aloft	Victorian
ravenous	vestry	pre-fabricated
accost	atheist	futility
anthropology	predecessor	beset
sustenance	stealthily	valiant
bough		

SECTION 3
(Chapters 8-11)

seiners	Evensong	radiance
ermine	leaden	taunt
matron	billeted	hegiras
committal	brailing	render
permeate	pantomime	gig
exultant	grouse	midwife
breech	constable	glade
Elizabethan	affirm	gill-net
abalone		

SECTION 4
(Chapters 12-17)

slovenly	prodigious	tenet
boisterous	phosphorescence	torrential
Yule	materialism	ominous
clergy	polyethylene	affable
rebuke	anthropologist	crimson
brogue	theology	inert
amenities	ill-kempt	enmity
rector	anachronism	communal
macabre		

SECTION 5
(Chapters 18-23)

propane	agony	leeward
communion	mite	navigable
haltingly	unseemly	garb
intensify	exodus	unctuous
pious	platitudes	fundamentals
anguish	poignancy	majestic
staunch	eddy	contour
fragrant	efficacious	cocky
inhospitable		

Vocabulary Activity Ideas

The vocabulary selected from *I Heard the Owl Call My Name* has been divided into five sections. For each section, you may wish to have students work together in cooperative learning groups to locate the vocabulary words and define them according to their context in the book.

Providing students with interesting vocabulary activities helps them understand the meaning of the words. This, in turn, allows students to integrate the vocabulary into their everyday language. Here are some suggestions for activities you might try using with your students. Be sure students always use the words with the same meanings as found in the book.

1. People of all ages like to make and solve puzzles. Ask your students to make their own **Crossword Puzzles** or **Wordsearch Puzzles** using the vocabulary words from the story.

2. Write sentences leaving blanks where the vocabulary words belong. Ask students to **Use Context Clues** to complete the sentences.

3. Have students work in cooperative learning groups to **Play Categories**. Have the groups create a chart with headings such as, Nouns, Verbs, and Adjectives. Have them sort the words and write them under the appropriate heading. After the groups have sorted all of the words, discuss the placement of each on the chart. Point out how words often have multiple meanings and may fit into more than one category.

4. Before students enter the classroom, write several vocabulary words on the chalkboard to be **Words of the Day**. As a warm-up activity, have students use a dictionary to locate the meanings of these words. Tell students to write the words and their meanings on notebook paper.

5. Have students create a **Literature-Generated Dictionary**. Have volunteers write the words and their definitions on chart paper or the chalkboard. Have students work together to alphabetize the words. Then have them use a notebook or journal to record the alphabetized words and their meanings. After recording the words and definitions, have students divide the words into syllables and write a sentence using each word.

6. Have students create a **Personal Vocabulary List**. Tell them to record any words from the story that they do not understand and the page numbers on which those words are found. Ask them to bring their list to class so students can review the context of the words and suggest definitions.

7. Have students play **Vocabulary Charades**. In this game, vocabulary words are acted out.

Quiz Time!

1. On the back of this paper, write a paragraph describing three important events from Section 1. Then complete the rest of the questions on this page.

2. Where does the young vicar go, and how does he get there?

    _____

    _____

3. Who gives the young vicar advice about how to relate to the people of the village?

    _____

    _____

4. How would you describe Jim Wallace?

    _____

    _____

5. What is important to the people of the village?

    _____

    _____

6. What did Mark Brian see in the eyes of the Indians?

    _____

    _____

7. Who died, and why hadn't he been buried?

    _____

    _____

8. In the old days, what did an Indian mother do when her child died?

    _____

    _____

9. How did the young RCMP officer react when he saw the weesa-bedó?

    _____

    _____

10. On the back of this paper, explain why Mark Brian left the burial service before everyone else, and describe what happened after he left.

10

Design Your Own Totem Pole

The Indians of the Northwest were master wood-carvers. The Europeans who first encountered them were amazed at the beautifully decorated masks, statues, and totem poles which the Indians created. Of course, the design on a totem pole represented more than just carving ability.

The carving of totem poles was related to tribal customs. Families were divided into totemic groups similar to clans, and the totem was almost like a clan ancestor. The Indians didn't believe they were descended from an animal. But the carvings of animals on the totem pole represented an ancestor's special relationship with an animal in a family legend.

When strangers visited from another village, first they would look at the totem poles in front of the houses to find one which belonged to members of their own totemic group. Then they could go to that home expecting to receive hospitality and protection.

Activity

Think about what animals could symbolize your family. Use the box on the right to design and color your own family totem pole. Then write a story to explain the significance of the animals on your totem pole.

Anticipation Guide

Your students will better understand and enjoy a book if they prepare for reading a book by relating situations in the story to their personal experiences. This is particularly true of a book such as *I Heard the Owl Call My Name*, because it has a setting with which most of them are probably not familiar.

Before students begin reading the book, show them a copy of it. Explain that they are going to read the book, but before they start they will give their opinions in response to some statements. Assure them that their answers will not be graded and that there are no right or wrong answers.

After students have completed the anticipation guide, discuss their answers. Then collect the guides so they can be reviewed after students have finished reading the story. When students have completed the book, ask them to respond to the statements on the anticipation guide again. When they are done, return their original guides and have them compare the two. Ask students to describe how reading the book changed their opinions.

Anticipation Guide

Respond to each of the following statements with **agree** or **disagree**.

1. Civilized people have the best ideas about how everyone should live, and they should work to change the way others live.

   _____

2. The length of one's life is more important than how one chooses to live.

   _____

3. People who continue to live as their ancestors did probably do so because they lack the intelligence to change their lifestyle.

   _____

4. There is a right way to do everything.

   _____

5. Only ignorant people are superstitious.

   _____

Myths

People have probably told stories since they first learned how to speak. Until written language was invented, storytelling was the way people passed down their beliefs and knowledge to their children and neighbors. Frequently, the storytellers used their tales to explain the world around them and describe how people should behave. We call these stories myths and legends.

Near the beginning of *I Heard the Owl Call My Name*, the bishop tells Mark, "The myths are the village." In other words, he recognized that the people of the village believed the myths were true stories. These beliefs formed the basis for their daily lives, as well as their traditions. Read the following myths which are based on oral stories told by the Indians of British Columbia.

Voice of the Spirit World

Once there was a beautiful place where the people had all the wild game, fish, and berries that they needed. In fact, the people had so much food, they could trade with other tribes. After awhile, however, the young people forgot the old ways of honoring nature by taking only what they needed. They began to take nature for granted. They took more food from the land and water than they could possibly use. They let the excess lay in waste and rot away. The elders warned that the Chief-in-the-Sky would be angry. But the young people foolishly disregarded these warnings.

The young people did not respect living things as they had been taught. Some of the young men found it amusing to catch a live salmon, cut slits in the fish's back, and put burning pitch into the slits. Then they put the salmon back into the water. It swam around in agony, as a living torch to illuminate the revelry of the young. Of course, the elders protested, but the young people paid no attention, laughing and jeering at the fears of their fathers.

When salmon season neared its end, the tribe began preparing for its annual winter ceremonies. Suddenly, they heard a loud noise in the distance which sounded like the beating of a drum. The elders became worried, but the young people laughed and cried in jest, "Aha! The ghosts awaken! They are going to have a feast, too! You silly old people are afraid of everything!" Sure enough, within a short time the noise died down. However, after a week or two the sound like beating drums began again and became louder and louder. Now even the young people felt frightened.

Suddenly, a horrible noise, like that of an overhead thunderclap, shook the ground. As quickly as the blink of an eye, the mountain tops split open and fire poured out until burning lava filled the rivers. The people tried to flee, but the forests burst into flames, so very few escaped. The spirit world had spoken, expressing its anger about the young people torturing the salmon.

Myths *(cont.)*

Raven and the Moon

One day Raven, the creator, heard that a fisherman and his daughter had a beautifully carved box in which they kept a bright light. They called this light the "moon." Raven wanted the moon so he decided to trick the fisherman's daughter. He changed himself into a baby and made it appear as though he had been abandoned in the forest. When the fisherman's daughter came to pick berries, she found the baby. She did not think the baby was very pretty because he had a long hooked nose like that of a bird's bill. But the fisherman's daughter took the baby home with her anyway. She treated him as if he were her own.

As soon as the boy could speak, he began asking for the moon. He would say, "Moon, moon, shining moon." Then one day the fisherman, who gave the boy everything he wanted, told his daughter, "Let the boy play with the moon."

The fisherman's daughter opened the beautifully carved box. Inside there was another box, more beautiful than the first. She opened box after box, each one smaller than the last and even more exquisitely carved. At last, she opened the last and smallest box. This one was the loveliest of all. It had a piece of silk thread tied around it. The fisherman's daughter untied the thread and opened the box. Suddenly, a bright white light filled the lodge. It was coming from the moon which was resting inside the box like a brilliant white ball. The fisherman's daughter threw the moon to the boy. He joyfully caught it and held onto it.

The boy did not remain content for long and soon began to cry. At first the fisherman and his daughter could not understand what the boy wanted. Eventually, they realized that he wanted to be able to see the stars in the night sky. So the fisherman made an opening in the top of the lodge especially for the boy.

As soon as the hole was made, the boy changed himself back into Raven. He grabbed the moon with his bill and flew out of the hole. He landed on the top of a mountain. From there, Raven hurled the moon up into the sky where it remains to this day.

Myths *(cont.)*

Hanging Hair

In the trees near a river there lived a lovely, gentle spirit named Hanging Hair. This spirit's job was to try to protect those who lived in the nearby village. The people often said that when the wind blew gently, they could see this spirit. One day Hanging Hair called for a great feast. She wanted to see if she could prevent the monster spirit, who controlled a dangerous whirlpool, from drowning the bravest young men of the village.

Hanging Hair invited all of nature's monster spirits. Some of them came in riding on the winds of a storm. Others came in calmly and gently. Each of the monster spirits possessed a special power, such as being able to fall off cliffs, freeze into pieces of ice, or burn like a forest fire, without ever being hurt. However, the monster spirits came peacefully into Hanging Hair's home under the water, for she was loved and respected by all of them. The spirits, including the one who controlled the dangerous whirlpool, took their places at the dining table.

Hanging Hair served her very best food, and the guests ate until they were full. When all the spirits had finished eating and were in a good mood, Hanging Hair explained that it was time for them to have more compassion for the people of the nearby village. She suggested that they reduce the powers of the monster spirit who controlled the whirlpool. All of the monster spirits agreed. They decided to shake the earth to divert the flow of some of the river's water. This would reduce the force of the whirlpool and eliminate the danger to the people. From that day forward the river flowed quietly and calmly.

Activity

Use the lines below to write what lessons you think were taught by these myths.

Voice of the Spirit World

_____

_____

Raven and the Moon

_____

_____

Hanging Hair

_____

_____

Reading Response Journals

Competent readers experience, or "get into," what they read. They relate to a story's characters in a very personal way. They respond to what they read with both their minds and their emotions. Teaching your students how to relate to the experiences they read about will help them better understand and enjoy the book.

Reading Response Journals provide an excellent way to help students personally experience what they read. In these journals, students can be encouraged to respond to the story in a number of ways. Try some of these ideas with your students.

- Ask students to create a journal for *I Heard the Owl Call My Name*. Tell students that the purpose of the journal is to allow them to record their thoughts, ideas, observations, and questions as they read *I Heard the Owl Call My Name*.

- Before students read a chapter, give them a question to think about while they are reading. Have them respond to the question in their journal. Sample questions for each chapter can be found on page 45.

- Have students use their journals to take notes on cultural or historical background information that you provide. These notes will enable students to better understand the context of story events.

- Vary the daily strategies you use to have students read the book. Strategies can include having students: take turns reading aloud; read silently; and follow along as you read aloud with expression. While reading, allow students to freely ask questions or make comments about the content of the story. Point out literary terms. Have students use their journals to record these terms, define them, and give examples from the book.

- Spend class time on the book so students know that reading it is important. Be sure students write in their journals on a daily basis.

- Have a special place in your classroom to keep the journals. This will serve two purposes. It will keep the journals in good condition over the time period that students are reading the book, and it will make the journals easily accessible to students. Let students know you consider the journals to be important. Encourage students to take the completed journals home to share with a family member.

Quiz Time!

1. On the back of this paper, write a paragraph to describe three important events from Section 2. Then complete the rest of the questions on this page.

2. What vegetable does Mrs. Hudson always serve the clergy, and why?

   _____

   _____

3. Name three characters described in Section 2.

   _____

   _____

4. Why didn't Mark want a new vicarage?

   _____

   _____

5. Who were Mark's first friends in the village?

   _____

   _____

6. What gift did Marta give to Mark?

   _____

   _____

7. List 3 reasons why the fable of the salmon is a very significant part of Section 2.

   _____

   _____

   _____

8. When did the Indians fish and hunt less than usual?

   _____

   _____

9. Why didn't the Indians want to talk when they were going on a hunt?

   _____

   _____

10. How did Calamity Bill get his nickname?

    _____

    _____

Breaking Bread

The bishop told Mark many useful things when Mark asked about the village. But he was wrong when he said that the villagers would not thank Mark for anything he did because they did not have a word for "thank you." Communication consists of more than just spoken language. Communication also lies in the expression on a person's face and in one's gestures. For example, Marta thanked Mark for his sensitivity with her eyes and by giving him small presents. One of the gifts she gave him was a fresh loaf of home-made bread. Giving Mark the loaf of bread was a very special gesture. It showed hospitality and was Marta's way of saying, "This bread is very special. It shows I care about you because I want to give you something into which I have put my time and effort."

Bread has often been called "the staff of life" because it is one of the most basic foods for people. Most societies in the world have some form of bread as one of their main foods. We usually think of bread as a soft, raised loaf made from grain of some kind. However, some breads are unleavened, which means they are flat rather than raised. Tortillas and pita bread are examples of flat breads.

As bread became readily available for people to buy from stores and bakeries, fewer families baked their bread at home. However, today bread machines make it much easier to bake bread. As a result, many people are beginning to make their own bread. With a bread machine, you simply put in the correct ingredients, wait awhile, and the bread will automatically mix itself, rise, and bake. Baking bread, with or without the help of this special machine, is a very rewarding activity because everyone enjoys eating the product. Below is a recipe for oatmeal bread which is easy to make. You might want to try it at home. If you do, be sure to follow kitchen safety rules.

Oatmeal Bread

You will need:

2 packages dry yeast
$1^{1}/_{2}$ cups (375 mL) boiling water
$^{1}/_{2}$ cup (125 mL) light molasses
1 tablespoon (15 mL) salt
$6^{1}/_{4}$ cups (1.5 L) white flour
$^{1}/_{2}$ cup (125 mL) warm water
1 cup (250 mL) rolled oats
$^{1}/_{3}$ cup (75 mL) shortening

2 slightly beaten eggs
Vegetable oil
Small bowl
Large mixing spoon
Two large loaf pans
Large mixing bowl
Towel

Directions: Moisten the yeast using the warm water. In a large bowl, carefully mix the boiling water, oats, molasses, shortening, and salt. Cool the mixture until it is lukewarm. Stir in 2 cups (500 mL) of flour and the eggs. Beat well. Then stir in the yeast mixture and beat well. Add half of the remaining flour and beat until smooth, then add all of the remaining flour. Mix thoroughly for about 10 minutes or until the mixture is smooth. Grease the top of the dough with a little vegetable oil, using a paper towel. Refrigerate for at least two hours.

After the dough has risen, divide it in half, and place each half into a greased loaf pan. Cover with a towel, and let the dough rise in a warm place until it doubles in size. Bake in the oven at 375°F (190°C) for about 40 minutes.

Portray a Character

In Chapter Three, the author introduces us to several of the characters in *I Heard the Owl Call My Name*, such as Marta Stephens, Mrs. Hudson, and the teacher. Usually an author tells you several things about a character, including a description of the character's appearance and actions. In this chapter, however, the author does not tell you much about what the characters look like.

There aren't many physical descriptions of the characters in *I Heard the Owl Call My Name*. This is because the most important thing about the people in this story is what they are like inside. The author shows this by telling what the character does and says.

The description of Mrs. Hudson is an example of how a person's actions are more important than her appearance. Mrs. Hudson is the matriarch of the village which means she is the oldest woman there. She's happy that a new vicar is there because it means that the bishop and other vicars will probably come to the village occasionally. She wants the bishop and the other vicars to visit because she will be in charge of all the younger wives, as she is the oldest. Mrs. Hudson will tell them what to do and what to prepare. She shows how little she likes white people in a very subtle manner. She plans to serve mashed turnips to the white men when they come, because she knows none of them will like mashed turnips. In other words, she wants their company because it gives her a chance to have control over white people. The description of Mrs. Hudson's actions lets you know who she is without knowing what she looks like.

Activity

Work with a group of four or five other students. Have each person take the part of a different character in Chapter Three. Study the description of the character you choose. Think about how that person acts and what he or she might say. Ask yourself what kind of person your character is.

Write a script in which your character describes himself or herself. Without naming your character, use the script you've written to tell the class about your character. Have the class try to guess which character you are portraying.

After all students have portrayed their characters, discuss the following questions:

1.   How important is physical appearance?

2.   How much can you tell about what a person is really like by the way he or she looks?

The Fable

A common type of story found in the literature of most cultures around the world is the fable. A fable is a story in which animals or objects act like people in order to teach a lesson. When animals or objects share human characteristics, it is called personification. The lesson taught in a fable is called a moral.

There is a fable told within the story *I Heard the Owl Call My Name.* It is told by the Indian character named Jim, and it is about the salmon. Jim calls the salmon "the swimmer." As he tells the fable, other events take place as well. For example, Mark, Jim, and Marta eat lunch.

The fable about the salmon goes like this: The swimmer passes the young of his own kind as they go out to sea. The young are afraid, but they want to swim down the river of life to the sea. The swimmer, who is now old, knows that it is time for him to return to the place of his birth. By the time the swimmer gets there, he is bruised and battered. He has had to make this difficult journey by swimming upstream against the strong current of the river and jumping over jagged rocks. A female who is swimming nearby has made the same arduous trip and is also close to death. She digs a seed bed and lays her eggs before she dies. The swimmer covers the eggs with milt, thus ending his life, which has been filled with courage and adventure. He has devoted his entire life to doing that which he was meant to do, and he dies triumphantly.

Activity

After studying the fable about the swimmer, answer the following questions.

1.   How does the swimmer behave like a person in this story?

      _____

      _____

2.   What lesson does this story teach?

      _____

      _____

      _____

3.   What do you think this story meant to the Indians
      who told it?

      _____

      _____

      _____

      _____

Poetize the Swimmer

A poem is often written to appeal to your emotions and your imagination. It can be written according to a certain structure relating to the kinds of words, rhythm, and meaning. Read the following poem.

Baby
Crawly, Creepy
Stretching, straining, striving
He's looking for a better way to travel
Stumbling, strengthening, strutting
Confident, capable
Walker

This poem is called a diamond poem because it is shaped like a diamond. This shape is part of the poem's structure. The kinds of words used in each line are another part of its structure. Read the following breakdown of the types of words used in each line.

Line 1—A noun
Line 2—Two adjectives (descriptive words) which describe the noun
Line 3—Three verbs (action words) which tell what the noun does
Line 4—A statement which shows that the noun is changing in some way
Line 5—Three verbs which tell what the noun does to change
Line 6—Two adjectives which describe the noun after it changes
Line 7—A new noun which renames the noun in line 1

Notice that the words in lines 2 and 6 all begin with the letter "c," and the words in lines 3 and 5 all begin with the letters "st." This is an additional kind of structure called **alliteration**. Alliteration is the repeated use of the same sound.

Activity

Re-read the story about the salmon. Pretend that you are the salmon. Try to imagine what it would feel like to be the salmon. Write a diamond poem about some aspect of your life as a salmon. Remember to show change occurring in the body of your poem and to finish with a noun reflecting the change that has occurred. Then draw pictures to illustrate your poem.

Quiz Time!

1. On the back of this paper, write a paragraph describing three important events from section 3. Then complete the rest of the questions on this page.

2. Why did villagers become uneasy when the young people returned from school?

   _____

   _____

3. Who owned a beautiful mask?

   _____

4. How did the villagers relive their deepest beliefs?

   _____

   _____

5. How would you describe the potlatch?

   _____

   _____

   _____

6. Why did Jim's mother make him stay in his room before he danced the hamatsa?

   _____

   _____

7. Gordon's family owned a mask. What happened to it?

   _____

   _____

8. Why did Keetah's family exile themselves?

   _____

   _____

9. Who said, '*What have you done to us? What has the white man done to our young?*' Why?

   _____

   _____

10. How did the villagers react to the death of Gordon's mother?

   _____

   _____

Papier-Mâché Masks

Ceremonial masks were very important to the Kingcome Indians. They were symbols of traditional life.

You can make a mask for yourself. Try to make your mask portray a characteristic such as humor, fierceness, or anger. Your mask does not have to be round. It can be any shape you wish.

Here is what you need for the project:

- large bowl or tray
- cooking oil
- mixing bowl for paste
- a large spoon or stick for stirring the paste
- strips of newspaper or paper towels
- wallpaper paste
- objects for forming features (examples: paper cups, thread spools, egg carton cups, toilet tissue spools, pieces of cardboard)
- Tempera paint and paintbrush

Here are the directions for the project:

Step 1: Carefully mix the wallpaper paste with water according to the directions on the package.

Step 2: Turn the large bowl or tray over so its bottom is facing up. Use cooking oil to grease the bottom.

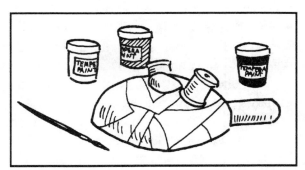

Step 3: Use the paste to apply two layers of newspaper or paper towel strips to the bottom of the bowl or tray.

Step 4: Add features, such as a nose, eyes, ears, and a mouth, using a variety of objects and pieces of cardboard.

Step 5: Cover the features with additional layers of paper strips and paste.

Step 6: Let your mask dry thoroughly. Then remove the bowl or tray and paint.

Tell a Story

People have told stories for a very long time. Before written language was invented, storytelling was the principal way people passed down their history, traditions, laws, and religious beliefs. In the village of Quee the Indian language is an oral one. No one even knows how words should be written. The young people are gradually losing their oral tradition as they leave the village and go into a world which emphasizes the written word.

People in our country once told stories more than they do today. Before the invention of radio and television, people told stories while sitting around the fireside. Stories were passed down from one generation to the next about family adventures and histories. One could know a lot about one's ancestors by the stories that were told about them. Storytelling became an art as people learned to dramatize and embellish the tales they told.

Today, many people devote a great deal of time to keeping the art of storytelling alive. For example, in Jonesborough, Tennessee, thousands of people get together each year to tell and hear stories at the National Storytelling Festival. The stories that are told at this festival, and others like it, include: anecdotes, fish stories, tall tales, ghost stories, tales of true events that are stranger than fiction, animal stories, tales of the supernatural, sad stories, stories of romance and adventure, and tales of famous historical figures. Any kind of story is apt to be told at a storytelling festival because the appeal of a good story remains strong.

Activity

Work together with two or three other students to select a story you would like to tell the class. Choose a story you know well. It can be a children's story or any other kind of story you wish. You may want to go to the library to look at a variety of stories. After you pick your story, decide who will tell each part. Then rehearse it together. Be sure to learn your story well, so you won't have to stop in the middle and try to think of what to say next. Find ways to make your story more exciting and interesting. For example, you may wish to use props as part of your storytelling. Props, short for properties, is a stage term used to indicate objects other than costumes or sets which are used in a play. Props can be used to make your story more realistic or more dramatic. Even an object as simple as a hat can add to your performance.

After your group feels comfortable telling the story, perform it for the class. Be sure to look around at your audience so you keep their attention. Relax and have fun telling your story.

Kingcome, British Columbia

I Heard the Owl Call My Name takes place in a village near Kingcome Inlet. This inlet is located in British Columbia, a beautiful Canadian Province in the far northwestern part of North America. Kingcome Inlet is one of the many bays along British Columbia's rocky coast. Not far from the shoreline, the land is covered with dense forest that is teeming with wildlife. Long ago several tribes of Indians made this area their home because of the abundant natural resources they found here.

The Indian tribes who lived near Kingcome Inlet did not need to know about agriculture since there were sources of food all around them. They survived by fishing, hunting, and gathering wild plants. The ocean and rivers provided an excellent place to find food. They were full of fish, seal, and whales. To tap this resource, the Indians built fishing boats, using trees from the forest. These remarkable boats, some of which measured over fifty feet in length and carried up to forty men, were made without using a single nail. They were so stable that the Indians were able to catch huge whales without capsizing.

In addition to fishing, the Indians got food by hunting and gathering. The forest was bursting with a variety of wildlife. There were large numbers of deer, bear, and caribou, as well as many smaller animals that were excellent sources of meat. Many wild plants could also be eaten. The Indians enjoyed berries, seeds, roots, and mushrooms.

These British Colombian Indians did not need to move from place to place searching for food. They found this area to be a desirable place to live. Not only did it have an ample supply of natural resources, but the nearby mountains provided a perfect means of protection from the raids of neighboring tribes. Consequently, they built the village of Kingcome near the mouth of the Kingcome River.

On the map below, locate the following and write the number for each from its location on the map. The first one is done for you.

_1_ British Columbia

_____ Kunaklini Glacier

_____ Alert Bay

_____ Queen Charlotte Strait

_____ Kingcome Inlet

_____ Sullivan Bay

_____ Silverthrone Mountain

_____ Vancouver Island

_____ Kingcome River

_____ Gilford Island

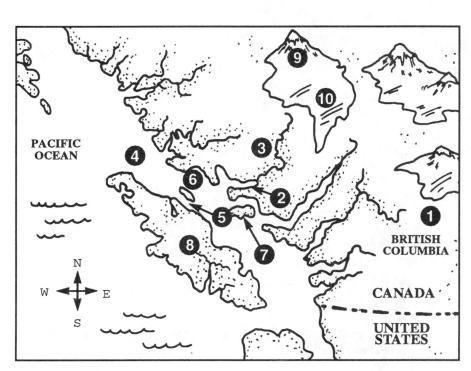

The Sale of the Giant Mask

In Chapter 8, the giant mask, which is the pride of Gordon's family, is described. *'See how thin it is. The modern ones are thick. ...It is my great-grandmother's hair.'* The mask was black with red lips and abalone eyes. *When Mark took it into his hands, he felt almost as if it held a strong, proud, living face, so beautifully was it carved. 'My father was offered three thousand dollars for it,' Gordon said, 'but we do not want to sell it.'* But the mask is sold, for only fifty dollars, to a white man who does not respect its importance to the village.

Choose two people from the list below, or others from the novel, and imagine that they are writing diary entries describing the sale of the mask and their feelings about the incident. Try to choose characters who will have varying points of view about it. Be ready to cite material from the book to support what you have written.

- Gordon
- Keetah
- Mark, the vicar
- the Bishop
- Mrs. Hudson
- Gordon's uncle

- Marta
- Jim
- Chief Eddy
- the white man who bought the mask
- an RCPM officer

- Keetah's sister
- Caleb
- Peter, the carver
- the teacher
- T.P., Gordon's grandfather

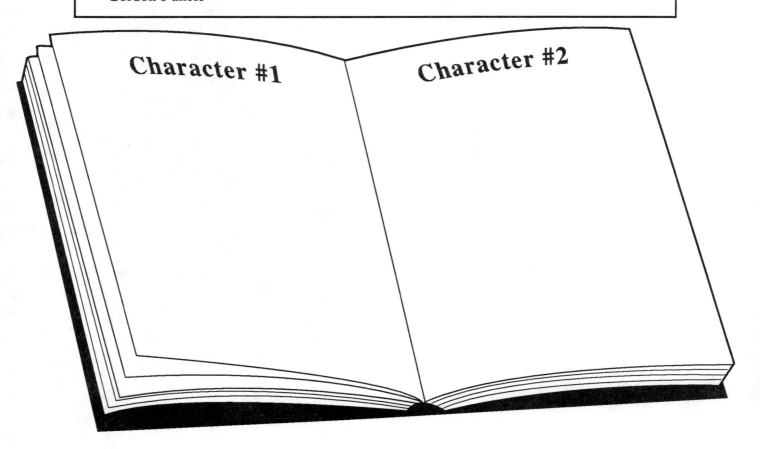

Character #1

Character #2

Quiz Time!

1. On the back of this paper, write a paragraph to describe three important events in section 4. Then complete the rest of the questions on this page.

2. Who wrote down stories of the past? Why was this task important?

    _____

    _____

    _____

3. What was delivered for Mark, and who assembled it?

    _____

    _____

4. What did the villagers do when the bishop came to the village?

    _____

    _____

5. Did the anthropologist respect the villagers? How can you tell?

    _____

    _____

    _____

6. How did the villagers "get back" at the anthropologist?

    _____

    _____

7. What advice did Mark give to the Indian boys who were leaving for the white man's school?

    _____

    _____

8. How did Ellie finally get to go away to school?

    _____

    _____

9. Where did the old villagers take Mark, and what did they do there?

    _____

    _____

10. On the back of this paper, describe how school affected Gordon.

Design a Canoe

The Indians of the Northwest still led a primitive lifestyle when Mark first went to the village. In general, they did not use metals except for small amounts of copper, which they obtained from the shipwrecked boats of Europeans. The Indians did not feel the need to use metals. They used their intelligence and creativity to make the most of their natural resources — wood and stone.

Not having metal tools meant that the Indians' tools were made exclusively from wood and stone. They did not have any nails, screws, or staples. Yet they were able to build marvelous boats, some measuring up to sixty feet (18m) long and eight feet (2.5 m) wide. The boats were extremely sea-worthy, allowing the Indians to catch not only a variety of fish, but whales as well.

Activity:

Combine your best problem-solving skills with your imagination to design a boat made of wood. Draw your design and write directions for how to make it. Your boat cannot use nails or any other type of metal fasteners. In addition, you must be able to assemble your boat without metal tools. However, you may use any of the natural resources that were also available to the Indians of British Columbia. Use the information in *I Heard the Owl Call My Name*. Feel free to consult reference books in the library. You can ask for help from your teacher or anyone you know who has information about boats. Have fun!

Supply the Crossword Clues

This crossword puzzle is probably different than most of the ones you have done. Here you are given the answers, and you must supply the clues.

Work together with three of four other students to complete this activity.

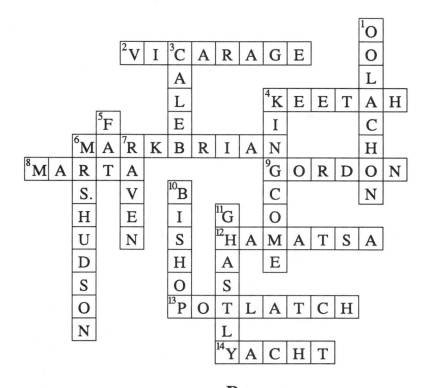

Across

2. _____
4. _____
6. _____
8. _____
9. _____
12. _____
13. _____
14. _____

Down

1. _____
3. _____
4. _____
5. _____
6. _____
7. _____
10. _____
11. _____

Synonyms

Have you ever noticed that good writers, such as Margaret Craven, are very clear and concise in the way they choose words? Authors pick their words to help create specific visual images for the reader. As a result, not just any word will do when it comes to writing a story!

As an example, think about the word "walk." There are many synonyms which mean almost the same as "walk," but they do not necessarily paint the same mental picture. Think of the picture you have in your mind when you read the following sentence:

>The man walked across the street.

How does your mental picture change when you substitute another word for "walk," as shown in the following sentences?

>The man sauntered across the street.
>The man staggered across the street.
>The man waddled across the street.

Each of the sentences shown above has a synonym for the verb "walk." However, you change the mental picture created by the sentence just by changing the verb! The first sentence which uses "walk" is rather vague, and you don't get a very clear picture of the rate or kind of walk the man has as he moves across the street. The other three sentences use verbs that give you a better mental picture of how the man walked as he went across the street. The verb "saunter" suggests that the man is walking in very leisurely way. The verb "stagger" suggests that the man is sick, injured, weak, or intoxicated and is having difficulty walking. The verb "waddle" suggests that the man is overweight and his body swings from side to side as he moves.

Activity

Using the columns below, list all the synonyms you can find for the words "walk" and "talk."

Walk	**Talk**
_____	_____
_____	_____
_____	_____
_____	_____
_____	_____
_____	_____

Important People

Mark and the villagers become important to each other. In fact, the villagers come to consider Mark to be one of them, and he is totally committed to them.

The author shows these feelings of mutual caring and commitment through events described in the story. For example, after returning from his patrol to other villages, Mark finds a loaf of fresh bread in the vicarage. In addition, the villagers share their food with Mark, tell him their most secret myths, and ask him to help them find a final resting place for their dead. They also offer to help him build a new vicarage. Mark, who begins to think like the villagers, politely responds to visiting white people but does not give in to their demands. He shows the Indians total respect and they show the same to him.

List three ways Mark shows respect for the villagers.

_____

_____

_____

Name someone you respect.

_____

List the reasons you respect this person.

_____

_____

_____

What qualities do you respect in a person?

_____

_____

_____

Is everyone worthy of respect? Explain why or why not.

_____

_____

_____

Why do you think respect is important?

_____

_____

For what would you like people to respect you?

_____

_____

_____

Quiz Time!

1. On the back of this paper, write a paragraph to describe three important events from section 5. Then complete the rest of the questions on this page.

2. Who died as Mark sat with him?

    _____

3. Why did Keetah return to the village?

    _____

    _____

4. How were family rights and ceremonies passed down to Jim?

    _____

    _____

5. Who saw death reaching out its hand and touching the cheek of the young vicar?

    _____

6. How would you describe the potlatch given in honor of Jim?

    _____

    _____

7. What did Mark mean when he said that in the village only the fundamentals counted?

    _____

    _____

8. When did Mark realize he was going to die soon?

    _____

    _____

9. What did Mark mean when he said, "I heard the owl call my name"?

    _____

    _____

10. How did Mark spend his last days?

    _____

    _____

    _____

Bake a Volcano

Many of the earth's mountains are volcanoes. About 850 of these volcanoes are active, which means they still erupt. Several volcanoes lie within a few hundred miles of Whoop-Szo, the mountain mentioned in *I Heard the Owl Call My Name*. Most of the earth's volcanoes lie in what is called the Ring of Fire, a belt which surrounds the Pacific Ocean. Some of these volcanoes are located on land, while others are in the ocean. Sometimes underwater volcanoes form mountains on the ocean floor or islands. For example, the Hawaiian Islands were formed by volcanoes, some of which still erupt.

The part of a volcano that can be seen is the mountain that is formed by volcanic activity. But there is a great deal more to a volcano that cannot be seen. Underneath the mountain part of the volcano, is a deep chamber of extremely hot liquid rock called magma. Hot gases build up pressure, forcing the magma through the layers of rock to the earth's surface. When the magma escapes to the surface, it is called lava. If the pressure from the gases builds rapidly, the consequence is an explosive eruption of lava. The eruption of Mount Saint Helens in Washington state in 1980 is an example of this kind of eruption. If the pressure builds slowly, there is a continuous ooze of lava. Eventually, the layers of lava cool, become solid, and gradually build up a cone for a mountain. Within the cone, there continues to be a central passage through which magma can flow if the pressure builds again. However, many volcanoes remain dormant, or asleep, most of the time. Some volcanoes have not erupted since long ago. They are thought to be extinct and are not expected to erupt again.

You can easily demonstrate how a volcano erupts with the following activity. Be sure to work under the direction of an adult and follow kitchen safety rules.

Here is what you need for the project:
    prepared pie crust
    cutting board
    fruit jam
    rolling pin
    oven preheated to 450°F (230°C)
    hot pot holders
    knife
    teaspoon
    round cookie cutters
    muffin pan

1.   Roll out the prepared pie crust, and cut two circles of dough for each cup in the muffin pan.
2.   Into each muffin cup, place one circle of dough, add a teaspoon of jam, and cover with another circle of dough.
3.   Press down the edges of the dough to seal each volcano.
4.   Carefully use the knife to cut a small hole in the top of each volcano.
5.   Turn on the oven light. Bake the volcanoes in the oven at 450°F (230°C) until the pressure builds up, and the jam erupts through the holes.

Build a Mountain

Just as Mark speaks the words, *'Therefore, with Angels and Archangels and with all the company of Heaven,'* a brilliant light suddenly fills the church, reflecting from the snow-covered top of Whoop-Szo, the noisy mountain. All the people raise their heads to see the brilliant light, and Mark feels as though all the difficulties of the winter have left with the promise of a new spring. Because of Whoop-Szo's importance to the villagers, this mountain figures prominently in their tribal mythology. The Indians tell stories about how they came to live near the mountain. They also tell how the spirit who lives in the mountain sent a slide to bury an enemy coming to attack the village.

The Indians told myths about the mountain because they did not understand how it came to be. Today we know that mountains are formed by reactions to movements of tectonic plates. Some mountains are made by the lava of volcanoes which appear along the edges of plates. Other mountains are made when plates collide and push up the layers of rock. The process of building mountains does not happen overnight. It takes place over a long period of time. Even today, mountains are constantly being formed on the earth's surface and under the ocean.

Now you can make a model of a mountain using layers of cardboard.

Activity

Work with three or four other students. Here is what you need for the project:

> pencil
> scissors
> several pieces of heavy cardboard
> one large piece of heavy cardboard to use as the base
> glue
> different colors of tempera paint
> paintbrush

1. Examine the picture of a contour map shown at the bottom of the page.
2. On the pieces of cardboard, draw different sized layers for your mountain. Make as many layers as you would like.
3. Cut out the layers.
4. Glue the layers down on the base, starting with the largest layer first and ending with the smallest layer.
5. After the glue has dried, paint each layer of your mountain using a different color.
6. Display your mountain for the class.

Cultural Beliefs About Numbers

People have held cultural beliefs about numbers for thousands of years. The Indians believed that the number four was special. According to the hamatsa myth, the cannibal man gobbled up four bodies and danced four times around the house. Four villagers left to bring water, but never returned, then the cannibal man came into the house four times on four nights.

Today, many people believe that the number seven is a lucky number because it is referred to many times in the Bible. One story says that God took seven days to create the world. Another story tells how Joshua defeated the city of Jericho. He told seven priests to carry seven trumpets. On the seventh day, these priests were to march seven times around the city blowing their trumpets so the walls of the city would fall. According to the story, the priests did as Joshua said, and the walls of Jericho fell.

Many groups of people have considered other numbers to be special, as well. The Mayans of ancient Mexico and Central America believed that each of the first thirteen numbers represented a god. The Babylonians had sixty gods, each of which was associated with one of the first sixty natural numbers. You could tell exactly how important a particular Babylonian god was by knowing its number. The god with the number one was the most important. In China the odd numbers represented life and heat, and the even numbers represented death and cold. Pythagoras, the Greek philosopher and mathematician, considered even numbers to be feminine and earthly and odd numbers to be masculine and heavenly. Our term the "square deal," meaning justice, came from the first square number, four. The number 5 has been used to represent marriage according to the following formula:

$$\begin{array}{r} 2 \text{ (the first female number)} \\ + 3 \text{ (the first male number)} \\ \hline 5 \text{ (marriage)} \end{array}$$

Activity

Take a survey of your parents, teachers, and friends by asking them the following questions. Then compare your answers to those of your classmates.

1.   Do you consider any number unlucky? If so, which one?

2.   Do you consider any number lucky? If so, which one?

3.   Would you fly on Friday the thirteenth?

4.   Would you stay in a hotel room with the number 1313?

The Meaning of Life

At the beginning of *I Heard the Owl Call My Name* you know that Mark is going to die within two years. This is something not even he knows. Death is often hard for people to accept. Some people seem to act as though they are never going to die. They may even believe they won't.

Strangely enough, while Mark's body is preparing to die, Mark's mind is learning what it really means to live. He comes to understand what the fundamentals of life really are. He makes friends with loneliness and death because he must confront it on a daily basis as part of his work in the village. Mark learns "enough of the meaning of life to be ready to die." He becomes like "the swimmer" in Jim's fable, who spends his time in the river of life doing the job he was made for and then dying, not in sadness, but in triumph.

Activity

Mark Brian was not a famous man, and he did not accomplish any miraculous deed. However, he won the hearts of the villagers, and they considered him to be one of them.

Today, the friends or relatives of a deceased person often place an article in the newspaper. This article is called an **obituary** and it is written in honor of the person who has died. An obituary often tells about the deceased person's life, what was important to him or her, and what was special about her or him.

At a funeral, the friends and relatives of the deceased person may give a **eulogy**. A eulogy is a public speech or written tribute given in honor of the person who has died.

Write either an obituary or a eulogy in honor of Mark Brian. Tell why his life was important and what he meant to the Indian people with whom he spent his last days. Tell why he will be missed and what he contributed to the lives of the people around him.

Any Questions?

After you finished reading *I Heard the Owl Call My Name*, did you have some questions that were left unanswered? Write a few of your questions here.

_____

_____

_____

_____

_____

_____

_____

_____

Work alone or in groups to prepare possible answers for the questions you have asked above and those written below. When you finish your predictions, share your ideas with the class.

What happened between Jim and Keetah? Did they have a happy marriage? How many children did they have? Did they always live in the village?

Did Gordon become a professional? If he did, what kind of professional did he become? Did he try to help the villagers after he got his education? Did he forget about his Indian ways and go on to completely embrace the white man's ways?

Who came to the village to take Mark's place? Did he learn from the way Mark had worked with the Indians? Did he learn from the Indians as much as Mark did?

Did the teacher ever decide to work with the villagers, or did he continue to hide from life and death? What caused him to be so afraid and so demanding?

What kind of service did the villagers have for Mark? Why did they ask the bishop and the other rectors to leave after the church service? In the days that followed, what kind of stories did the Indians tell about Mark? Did Mark become the subject of any myths? Where was he buried? Do you believe he rested in peace?

Did the young people continue to leave the village until everyone was gone, or did a small group stay under the leadership of Jim and Keetah? If some of the Indians stayed in the village, were they able to keep out the influences of the white man's world?

Book Report Ideas

There are a variety of ways you can report on a book. After you have finished reading *I Heard the Owl Call My Name*, choose a method of reporting that interests you. You can do a traditional book report, or you may choose a way to report using your own idea, an idea suggested by your teacher, or one that is listed below.

- **Write a Poem**

Write a poem about a character or a myth that is described in *I Heard the Owl Call My Name*. It can be any type of poem you choose. For example, you may want to make your poem a ballad which is a story told in verse.

- **Write a Myth**

Write a myth to explain something about the way the world works. In your myth, you may include supernatural characters, characters who represent your ancestors, and special heroic characters who demonstrate why you hold a certain belief to be true.

- **Tell a Story**

Choose a myth or legend which particularly interests you, practice telling it, and perform it for the class. You might pretend to be a character from the book as you tell the story. Use props, such as posters, pictures, totem poles, costumes, or masks, to help dramatize your story. If you have access to music which would go well with your myth, you might want to use it to help you dramatize your story.

- **Give a Demonstration**

Give a demonstration to further explain something from the book. You might choose to give a science demonstration about the life of the salmon or the killer whale. You might decide to demonstrate how the Indians made a totem pole or a wooden canoe.

- **Produce a Skit**

Pick an important event described in *I Heard the Owl Call My Name*. Work cooperatively with one or more friends, to write, produce, and perform a skit about this event.

- **Interview a Character**

With the help of a friend, write and conduct an interview with one of the characters in *I Heard the Owl Call My Name*. One person should play the part of the interviewer and the other person should play the character being interviewed.

- **Make a Photo Album**

Draw a series of pictures to represent photographs showing important events in the story. Then make an album for your pictures.

- **Design a Movie Advertisement**

Pretend that *I Heard the Owl Call My Name* is going to be made into a television movie. Use pictures and words to design an advertisement which encourages people to watch this wonderful movie.

- **Write a Letter**

Pretend you are one of the villagers, and write a letter of condolence to Mark Brian's sister. In your letter, tell about the impact Mark had on your village, and, in particular, tell of the impact he had on your life. In your letter, describe specific events from the story to illustrate the kind of person Mark was and explain why he will be missed so much.

Research Ideas

Describe three things in *I Heard the Owl Call My Name* about which you'd like to learn more.

1. _____

2. _____

3. _____

As you read *I Heard the Owl Call My Name* you came across geographical locations, mythology, cultural beliefs, lifestyles, and foods which you've probably never heard of before. Learning about cultural, scientific, and historical information which relate to important concepts in the book will help improve your comprehension of the story.

Choose one or more topics from your list above or from the list provided below. Work with a group or by yourself to research each topic you have chosen. Give an oral presentation to share your research with the class.

- Indian life
    - Marriage customs
    - Puppets
    - Arts and crafts
    - Clothing
    - Mythology and legends
    - Dance
    - Totem poles
    - Masks
    - Family life
    - Whale hunters
    - Slavery in Indian villages
    - Warfare
    - Music
    - Basket weaving
    - Tools
    - Types of gods
    - Significance of nature
    - Significance of the beaver
    - Significance of the raven
    - Significance of the bear
    - The shaman
    - Potlatch
    - Languages
    - Shell money

- Animals
    - Salmon
    - Killer whales
    - Candlefish
    - Shellfish
    - Seals
    - Sea lions
    - Diving ducks

- The Northwest
    - History of British Columbia
    - Explorers of the Northwest
    - Kwakiutl Indians
    - Plant foods native to the Northwest
    - George Vancouver
    - Hudson's Bay Company
    - Origin of the Northwest Indians
    - Eskimos/Innuit
    - Principal tribes

- Boat-making
- Astronomy
- Canoeing
- Types of fishing nets
- Obsidian
- Woodcarving
- Harpoons
- Fur trading
- Whaling
- Stone carving
- Life in the Stone Age
- Bark textiles

Storytelling Potlatch

The Indians described in *I Heard the Owl Call My Name* made excellent use of the abundant natural resources of the area. These resources made it possible for the Indians to have a good life. As a result, the Indians' ceremonial life often revolved around these resources. They treated all aspects of nature with respect and never took more than they really needed. They honored animals, such as salmon, bears, beavers, seals, and sea birds, by creating wood and stone carvings of them. The Indians told myths about nature. These myths were used to teach the young people to conserve, to respect their animal friends, and to share with their neighbors.

The Indians' major ceremony was the potlatch festival. This festival was a time for storytelling and a way for the Indians to gain social prestige by giving away their wealth. A wealthy man in the village was expected to give about three potlatches during his lifetime. At these potlatches, this man might give away most of what he owned. Those who were invited to the potlatch were obligated to invite the rich man to a potlatch in return. As a guest at other potlatches, the rich man might receive more than he had given. As a result, this man could become richer rather than poorer.

You can have your own potlatch festival. Instead of giving away material goods, you will bring your best story to share at the potlatch. You can write any type of story and it can be as long as you like. Remember a story does not have to be long to be interesting or entertaining.

Work with a small group to plan a potlatch for your class. On a separate sheet of paper, make a chart with the following headings: People to Invite, Activities, Displays, Schedule, Preparations Needed. Have the members of your group brainstorm a list of ideas for each category.

Make copies of the potlatch invitation on page 41 to invite parents, teachers and students from other classes, and community members.

You may wish to use some of the following ideas for the displays and events at your potlatch.

Displays
    Papier-mâché masks
    Totem poles
    Illustrated poems
    Fables created by the class
    Posters showing different beliefs about numbers
    Posters showing results of number survey
    Models of mountains

Events
    Storytelling contest or sharing
    Picnic or classroom luncheon
    Dramatic portrayal of characters from book
    Demonstration showing how to bake bread
    Demonstration of how volcanoes erupt
    Skits dramatizing Indian myths

Potlatch Invitation

Trace the invitation shown on this page to make invitations to your storytelling potlatch. Cut along the solid line and fold along the dotted line of each invitation. Then neatly write the invitations and decorate them. Hand deliver the invitations to the people you want to come to your storytelling potlatch.

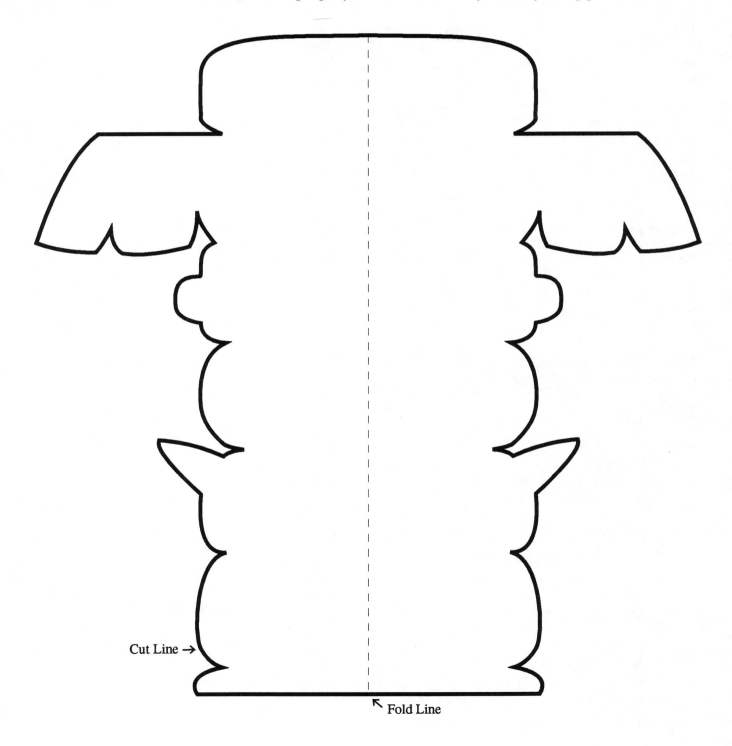

Cut Line →

↖ Fold Line

Unit Test

Matching: Write the correct letter on the line to match the descriptions of the characters with their names.

1. _____ Marta
2. _____ Caleb
3. _____ Jim
4. _____ Gordon
5. _____ Mark Brian
6. _____ Keetah
7. _____ Sam
8. _____ Calamity Bill
9. _____ Mrs. Hudson
10. _____ The RCMP
11. _____ Gordon's mother
12. _____ T.P.

A. Got drunk and lost the washing machine in the river
B. Makes mashed turnips for white people
C. Heard the owl call his name
D. Is the village midwife
E. The old canon
F. Rode his gear down the mountain
G. Wanted to become his people's first professional
H. Issued burial permits
I. Died in childbirth
J. Said the final words at Mark's funeral
K. Wanted to marry Keetah
L. Returned to the village

True of False: Write true or false in the blanks below.

1. _____ Mark tried to get the villagers to give up their beliefs and accept his.
2. _____ When Keetah went away to school, she gave up her old ways to become like the white people.
3. _____ The teacher wanted to make life easier for the villagers.
4. _____ Mark never knew he was going to die.
5. _____ From the very beginning, the villagers respected Mark, because he showed respect for them.

Short Answer: Using the space provided, write a brief response to each question.

1. Who accompanied Mark when he went around on his patrol?_____

2. In what ways did Mark's life change after he started living in the village? Describe three of these.

_____

_____

_____

3. What is the name of a big feast in which things are given away?_____

4. How does Ellie finally get to go away to school?_____

_____

5. What is the hamatsa?_____

Essay: Pretend you are either Marta or Jim. Write a biography about Mark Brian and tell about the years he spent in the village. To make Mark really "come alive" in your biography, include some of the following: visual imagery of the village and its people; a description of some of Mark's everyday activities; some generalizations about the kind of person Mark was.

Essay Challenge: Try to include dialogue (conversation) in your essay.

Response

Explain the meaning of these quotations from *I Heard the Owl Call My Name*.
To the teacher: Choose the appropriate number of quotes to which your students should respond.

Chapter 1
'The Indian knows his village and feels for his village as no white man for his country, his town, or even for his own bit of land.'

Chapter 2
'...Do not look back. Do not turn your head. Walk straight on. You are going to the land of the owl.'

Chapter 3
He did not like the Indians and they did not like him.

Chapter 4
'I'd rather come down on the vicarage than have the vicarage come down on me.'

Chapter 5
'Come, Swimmer,' he said. 'I am glad to be alive now that you have come to this good place where we can play together. Take this sweet food. Hold it tight, younger brother.'

Chapter 6
Both knew there was friendship between them now, forged without words and needing none.

Chapter 7
'They are not simple, or emotional, they are not primitive.'

Chapter 8
'They do not remember the myths, and the meaning of the totems. They want to choose their own wives and husbands.'

Chapter 9
She was a pretty girl, her hair carefully cut and waved, her fingernails red, the heels of her slippers very high.

Chapter 10
'When he tires of her, she will be alone in a world for which she has had no preparation.'

Chapter 11
'You suffered with them, and now you are theirs, and nothing will ever be the same again.'

Chapter 12
She said, 'Forgive me because I seek your dress. I will not leave you naked', and she told the tree what she would make from the bark—a blanket, and a pillow for her baby's head.'

Chapter 13
'Since I was a girl,' she announced, 'I have been interested in the culture of the Quackadoodles.'

Chapter 14
" 'You will make a joke of it. You'll laugh and you'll say, 'What's the matter, paleface?' "

Chapter 15
'The myth is a story. There is no harm in the myth, and I will tell it to you.'

Chapter 16
He saw Gordon with a surge of pride and a twinge of anguish.

Chapter 17
'Very soon only the old will be left and a very few others, and when the old die, the others will leave.'

Chapter 18
No woman said, 'I am sorry. I have only enough fuel for my own family.'

Chapter 19
'To let him go. To keep a part of him here in his village with his own people....'

Chapter 20
It was death reaching out his hand, touching the face gently, even before the owl had called the name.

Chapter 21
How would he live again in the old world he had almost forgotten, where men throw up smoke screens between themselves and the fundamentals...?

Chapter 22
'And when you build Keetah a house, let her plan it with you. And don't leave her alone in the village too long.'

Chapter 23
Past the village flowed the river, like time, like life itself, waiting for the swimmer to come again on his way to the climax of his adventurous life, and to the end for which he had been made.

Conversations

Work in size-appropriate groups to write and perform the conversation that might have occurred in one of the following situations.

- Keetah and Jim plan their home together. (2 persons)

- Sam and his wife discuss Ellie's progress in school. (2 persons)

- The bishop and Mrs. Hudson discuss the new menu after Mark's funeral. (2 persons)

- Keetah and Jim reminisce about Jim's friendship with Mark. (2 persons)

- Jim tells the elders about the slide that killed Mark. (3-4 persons)

- Jim and Keetah tell their son about Mark's stay in the village. (3 persons)

- The bishop tells the new vicar of Mark's success in the village. (2 persons)

- The elders tell the guests at the next potlatch about how the villagers responded to Mark's stay in the village. (3-4 persons)

- Gordon returns to the village and asks Jim about the slide. (2 persons)

- Mrs. Hudson helps Keetah plan her wedding. (2 persons)

- T.P., Chief Eddy, and Mrs. Hudson plan the next potlatch. (3 persons)

- Mrs. Hudson confesses to the bishop why she used to serve mashed turnips to the white men and why she stopped. (2 persons)

- Keetah tells her daughter about her life as a young girl in the village. (2 persons)

- Jim discusses with his son the importance of living harmoniously with nature. (2 persons)

- Marta and Keetah reflect on the positive changes Mark brought to the village. (2 persons)

- Mark discusses with the teacher the real meaning of life. (2 persons)

- Gordon finds the white man who took the family's mask and tries to convince him to return it. (2 persons)

- The four Indian boys, who went to the white man's school, discuss the things Mark taught them about living in the white man's world. (4 persons)

- The bishop and the anthropologist discuss her behavior in the village. (2 persons)

- The teacher and the party from the yacht discuss the village. (3-4 persons)

- The bishop and a movie producer discuss making a movie about Mark's life in the village. (2 persons)

Sample Response Journal Questions

Section 1

Chapter 1:
Why did Caleb tell Mark not to feel sorry for himself for being sent to a remote church? What does Mark learn about the Indians on his way to Kingcome? What did the bishop tell Mark about the village?

Chapter 2:
What does Mark notice about the villagers as he meets them? Who was the Weesa-bedó and what does Mark have to do for him? How do the villagers feel about death? Describe the RCMP's reaction to the Weesa-bedó.

Section 2

Chapter 3:
Why was Mrs. Hudson pleased that there would be a new vicar in the village? Who was Sam?

Chapter 4:
Describe the vicarage. How do the villagers treat Mark? Who were Mark's first friends in the village, and how did he meet them? How did Mark's first Sunday go?

Chapter 5:
How do Mark and Jim finally become friends? Describe the story of the swimmer.

Chapter 6:
Describe Mark's first hunt.

Chapter 7:
What problems did Mark have during his first winter? How did Calamity Bill get his nickname? Who do you think was the Cedar-man, and how might he have gotten his name?

Section 3

Chapter 8:
Why do the villagers resent the young people when they come home from the white man's school? About what was Mrs. Hudson worried?

Chapter 9:
Describe the potlatch. How had the potlatches changed over the years that Jim had lived? How did Gordon's family lose the mask and how did they react to the loss?

Chapter 10:
How did the villagers prepare for the coming of the óolachon? What do the villagers believe about their relationship with nature? What happened to Keetah's sister?

Chapter 11:
What is different about the way the RCMP handled the burial certificate of Gordon's mother and the way he handled the death certificate of the Weesa-bedó? Describe the service which was held for Gordon's mother. What did Chief Eddy tell Mark about the new vicarage, and how has this changed from when Mark first arrived?

Section 4

Chapter 12:
How did the villagers build a new vicarage? Why was Mrs. Hudson unhappy about the rectors coming to the village this time, and how did she react? How did the villagers celebrate the new vicarage?

Chapter 13:
Why did Mark refuse to take the Americans back to their yacht? How did the anthropologist show her disrespect for the Indians?

Chapter 14:
What did Mark and Jim teach the boys on their way to the white man's school? How has the village changed Mark from the way he had been with his old friends? Why had Sam's wife gotten angry with him, and what did she do about it?

Chapter 15:
What problem did the village elders ask Mark to help them solve? What was the hamatsa?

Chapter 16:
How has Gordon changed? What is Mark's relationship with the village now?

Chapter 17:
How is the cedar important to the villagers? How and why does Caleb think the village is going to change?

Section 5

Chapter 18:
What does Mark do at Calamity Bill's house? What does Mark promise to do in the spring?

Chapter 19:
Why does Keetah return to the village? What does Jim mean when he says, "A child is always welcome"?

Chapter 20:
What does Marta see when she looks at Mark? What has Mark learned by living in the village?

Chapter 21:
How did Mark feel about leaving the village? What does Mark do to Calamity Bill? How has Mark's feeling about time changed? Why did Marta only say, "Yes, my son," when Mark told her that he heard the owl call his name?

Chapter 22:
What does Keetah ask Mark to do and why? How does Mark counsel Jim about Keetah when he is no longer there?

Chapter 23:
Why did Keetah pray for both Jim and Mark? How does Mrs. Hudson change her usual plan for feeding a large number of guests, including white men? Describe the role of the white teacher throughout the book.

Bibliography

Reference and Resource Books

American Red Cross. *Standard First Aid and Personal Safety*. (Doubleday and Company, Inc., 1979)

Baker, Mary L. *Whales, Dolphins, and Porpoises of the World*. (Doubleday and Company, Inc., 1987)

Better Homes and Gardens. *Better Homes New Cookbook*. (Meredith Publishing Company, 1962)

Boy Scouts of America. *Indian Lore*. (Boy Scouts of America, 1992)

Burland, Cottie. *North American Indian Mythology*. (The Hamlyn Publishing Group Ltd.)

Detroit Free Press. "How the Earth Works." (San Jose Mercury News, January 19, 1993)

Flegg, Graham. *Numbers, Their History and Meaning*. (Schocken Books, 1983)

Gale Research. *Contemporary Authors, Volume 17*. (Gale Research Company, 1982)

Gale Research. *Contemporary Literary Criticism, Volume 17*. (Gale Research Company, 1981)

Gardner, Robert. *The Whale Watchers' Guide*. (Julian Messner, 1984)

Hogan, Paula Z. *The Salmon*. (Raintree Children's Books, 1979)

Lewis, Norman. *The New Roget's Thesaurus*. (G.P. Putnam's Sons, 1986)

National Association for the Preservation and Perpetuation of Storytelling. *Best Loved Stories Told at the National Storytelling Festival*. (National Storytelling Press, 1991)

Random House. *The Random House Children's Encyclopedia*. (Random House, 1991)

Westenberger, Theo, photographs by. *For Native American Dance, Standing Room Only*. (Smithsonian Associates, February, 1993)

Fiction

George, Jean Craighead. *Julie of the Wolves*. (Dell, 1986)

Highwater, Jamake. *Legend Days*. (HarperCollins Children's Books, 1984)

Hughes, Monica. *Hunter in the Dark*. (Avon, 1984)

O'Dell, Scott. *Island of the Blue Dolphins*. (Houghton Mifflin, 1990)

Thomasma, Ken. *Soun Tetoken: Nez Perce Boy Tames a Stallion*. (Baker Books, 1989)

Answer Key

Page 10

1. Accept appropriate responses.
2. Mark goes to a remote Indian village in British Columbia by boat.
3. The old canon gives advice to Mark.
4. Jim is about twenty-seven years old. He wears a fisherman's dark trousers and jacket with gum boots hanging over his shoulder. He carries his belongings in a cardboard box tied with string. He is patient, proud, and sad.
5. Nature, traditions, and myths are important to the villagers.
6. Mark sees deep sadness.
7. The Weesa-bedó. He had not been buried, because the RCMP had not yet been to the village to issue a burial permit.
8. She would kick the body three times, saying, "Do not look back. Do not turn your head. Walk straight on. You are going to the land of the owl."
9. He got sick.
10. Accept appropriate responses which show that Mark realized that the villagers wanted him to leave, so they could conduct their traditional burial service without him.

Page 17

1. Accept appropriate responses.
2. She serves mashed turnips, because white people don't like them.
3. Answers should include three of the following: Calamity Bill, Mrs. Hudson, Marta Stephens, Sam, Ellie, Peter the woodcarver, the teacher.
4. He didn't know how to get the vicarage to the village or how to put it up. He planned to patch up the old one.
5. The little girl and boy were Mark's first friends.
6. She made a hat for him.
7. The fable shows the close relationship between the Indians and nature, how the Indian considered nature's creatures to be equal to people, and how people who live life as they were meant to can die triumphantly.
8. The Indians fished and hunted less during the winter.
9. They did not want to scare the animals, causing them to hide.
10. Calamity Bill got his nickname when, in the course of cutting his timber, he rode his gear down the mountain three different times.

Page 22

1. Accept appropriate responses.
2. The young people have changed. They have forgotten many of the traditions and have adopted white people's ways.
3. Gordon's family owned a beautiful mask.
4. The villagers relived their beliefs through their dances at the potlatch.
5. There was music and dancing with everyone dressed in ceremonial clothing. Dances lasted three hours. There were 26 characters, each wearing a different mask. After the dancing, there were refreshments. Then gifts were given by the host to all the guests except for those in his own family.
6. Because the young man bewitched by the cannibal spirit must not be seen until he returns from the woods.
7. The white boyfriend of Keetah's sister got the men drunk and Gordon's uncle sold it to him for fifty dollars.
8. They were ashamed about the mask being sold.
9. Mrs. Hudson said this because she felt the influence of the white man on the Indian youth was leading to the end of their traditional way of life, as evidenced by the sale of the mask.
10. The villagers closed the bedroom door until the RCMP could come. There were no professional wailers, because she had not wanted them. The women washed and dressed the body, put it in the box, and put the box in the church. The women prepared food for the guests from other villages, and they all took the body to the burial ground and buried it. They went ahead with their normal routines, because death was part of everyday life for them.

Page 25

1	British Columbia
10	Kunaklini Glacier
5	Alert Bay
4	Queen Charlotte Strait
2	Kingcome Inlet
6	Sullivan Bay
9	Silverthrone Mountain
8	Vancouver Island
3	Kingcome River
7	Gilford Island

Answer Key *(cont.)*

Page 27

1. Accept appropriate responses.

2. Keetah wrote the stories down so they would not be forgotten.

3. Parts for a new vicarage were delivered and the villagers helped Mark assemble it.

4. The villagers came to church and had their babies baptized and their children confirmed, they went to the doctor for various aches and pains, and they barbecued salmon and danced traditional dances.

5. No, she was very insensitive and rude to them, and she called them "quackadoodles."

6. They would not tell her the story of the raven, they took her in a boat through very rough water so she would get seasick; and they let her step out of the boat into the water that was up to her armpits.

7. He taught them the white man's words of courtesy, such as, May I..., Excuse me, etc.; how to shake hands; and what to do if someone called them names.

8. Sam made a large sum of money from fish that he had caught. He spent most of the money on liquor and the rest of it on a washing machine. He lost the washing machine in the river. As a result, his wife was so angry that she beat him over the head with a skillet and locked him out of the house. She wouldn't let him back in the house until he agreed to let Ellie go to school.

9. The old villagers took Mark to the ancient burial ground. Together they dug a new mass grave and transferred all the remains of their dead to it. Then they held a brief service over the new grave.

10. At first Gordon didn't do well, then he began studying hard and planned to do two years' work in one. He came back to the village wearing white men's clothes and ignoring Indian customs. He decided to become a professional.

Page 28

Techniques used by the Indians to build their boats included: steaming and soaking wood, cutting wood with stone axes, stretching and shaping wet wood on frames, sanding with sandstone and sharkskin. Accept any reasonable solutions.

Page 29

Across

2. Home for a vicar
4. Plans to marry Gordon
6. Name of the young vicar (two words)
8. Person who delivers babies, bakes bread, makes hats, earth mother
9. Man who goes away to school to become a professional
12. Dance of the cannibal
13. Celebration for the giving away of personal wealth

14. The type of boat used by rich Americans

Down

1. Candlefish
3. Name of the old canon
4. Name of village
5. Kwakiutl delicacy
6. Proud, old lady (two words)
7. A bird who is a trickster
10. Sends Mark to the village
11. Anthropologist says this

Page 32

1. Accept appropriate answers.
2. Calamity Bill died as Mark sat with him.
3. Keetah wanted to retain her Indian way of life and return to her people.
4. The family rights and ceremonies were passed on to Jim at a potlatch.
5. Marta saw death touching the cheek of the young vicar.
6. Answers can include: a great feast, songs chanted, dances of the fish and the dog, the hamatsa, refreshments, the giving of gifts, and leaving on the third day.
7. Mark meant that the villagers cared only about the essentials of life: food, shelter, and caring for each other.
8. Mark realized that he was going to die when Marta confirmed his suspicions after the Bishop had spoken with him.
9. He meant that he was going to die.
10. He helped others spread Calamity Bill's ashes; he helped the Scottish people pull the rafts; and he searched for a lost logger.

Page 42

Matching

1. D	5. C	9. B
2. E	6. L	10. H
3. K	7. A	11. I
4. G	8. F	12. J

True or False

1. False
2. False
3. False
4. False
5. True

Short Answer

1. Jim joined Mark on his patrol.
2. Accept appropriate responses. Possible answers include: there were no modern conveniences, people had more respect for each other, and myths governed the Indians' way of life.
3. The potlatch was the big feast at which material wealth was given away.
4. Her father got drunk and lost the washing machine in the river. As a result, her mother got so angry she wouldn't let him back in the house until he agreed to let Ellie go to school.
5. The hamatsa is the cannibal dance.

Essay

Accept appropriate answers which include specific details from the story, with extra credit for using dialogue.

48